Killing Time

Simon Armitage was born in West Yorkshire in 1963. In 1992 he was a winner of one of the first Forward Prizes, and a year later was the *Sunday Times* Young Writer of the Year. In 1994 he received a major Lannan Award. He works as a freelance writer and broadcaster, has written extensively for radio and television, and lectures in creative writing at Manchester Metropolitan University and the University of Iowa.

In 1999 the Poetry Society appointed Simon Armitage as poet in residence with the New Millennium Experience Company, which commissioned the writing of a one-thousand-line poem. *Killing Time* is the result of that commission.

Broadcast by Channel 4 on New Year's Day, 2000, *Killing Time* is also a full-length film, written by Simon Armitage and produced by Century Films.

SIMON ARMITAGE

Killing Time

faber and faber

First published in 1999
by Faber and Faber Limited
3 Queen Square WC1N 3AU

Typeset by Faber and Faber Ltd
Printed in England by Clays Ld, St Ives plc

A CIP record for this book is
available from the British Library

ISBN 0-571-20360-4
ISBN 0-571-20461-9 (limited edition)

Thanks are due to Susan Roberts, Brian Hill, David Godwin,
Chris Meade and Andrea Petch. – S.A.

10 9 8 7 6 5 4 3 2

A man strolls past the town hall
　　　　wearing a sandwich-board for a coat,
and it ain't for the next closing-down sale,
　　　　or the time of the next coach,

and it ain't for the price of a fake tan,
　　　　or bringing the government down,
or happy hour, or two-for-one,
　　　　or the circus coming to town,

or a secret truth that God knows,
　　　　or the end of the world being nigh,
it says NO NEWS IS GOOD NEWS,
　　　　but it don't say why.

Killing Time

There's a new freak in the ape-house,
some monkey gone wrong,
loud-speakers for earlugs,
a microphone tongue,

fibre-optics for body hair,
a mouse for a hand,
a fax-machine derrière,
a joystick gland,

two screens for eyeballs,
a microchip brain,
a power-point in its navel
for batteries or mains.

It has no nerves or tear-ducts,
no spleen and no heart,
it has no hang-ups or secrets,
just a huge appetite.

First they tried it on porridge oats,
then they tried it on rusks,
they tried Black Forest gateaux,
threw it a few dried crusts,

they tried everything on the shelf,
they even tried it on booze,
but the thing wasn't itself
till they fed it the news.

The news — that's what the monkey loved,
it ate like there was no tomorrow,

3

had a particular taste for anything live
and a thirst for sorrow.

So they left no stone unturned,
put fingers in every pie,
left no darkness unwormed,
let no sleeping dogs lie.

Daily it needed three square meals,
liked to be fed with a spoon,
wanted the meaty bits chopped up small,
once nearly choked on a bone.

Sometimes they had to spin news out,
sometimes they let news rot,
it was piled on a plate through famine or drought,
newsworthy or not.

Then they all sat down at the monkey's feet,
switched on and tuned in.
After booting up with a virtual fart,
it flickered, and started to sing.

Meanwhile, the lights on Oxford Street this year
        ask us to stop and think
not of Christ in his crib or reindeers hauling a sleigh
        but a chemically-inferred orange drink
and the nation's best-known brand of frozen peas,
        frozen straight from the pod.
And couples walk its golden mile, brides and grooms on the aisle
        of the church where money is God.
Back where, back when, Christ was a painted clothes-peg
        in an After Eight box;
Mary the Tiny Tears doll and Joseph the Action Man
        knelt with the sheep and the ox
in the shape of a fun-fur teddy and porcelain dog
        from the mantelpiece, and all
were lit by a single flame from a nite-lite candle
        floating in a glass bowl
within the manger of an upturned packing case with a window hole.
        And it had the right feel,
even if one version of Christmas compared to another
        is no more or less real.
But tonight the bright star over the Middle East is the burn
        of a cruise missile homing in,
and on satellite TV we watch a game-show host
        disguised as an anchorman for CNN
go live to some security camera on an embassy roof
        which turns like an owl's head
as tracer-bullets rise like Amaretti papers aflame
        before the connection goes dead.
And although these are the opening shots of operation Desert Fox,
        not the Ryder Cup,
we have men on the fairway pointing at divots and craters
        where objects were blown up,

and although this isn't the old course at St Andrews
     but the Persian Gulf,
we have men on the ground, in the field, describing in terms
     of stroke-play golf
how laser-guided missiles were teed-off from abroad
     and made it through radar and flak
to find a good lie in a barracks or bunker
     this close to the flag.
And a well-shod president walks to the camera to say why
     we should put in the boot,
and when that happens, a well-dressed prime minister
     usually follows suit.
It's best to believe in equanimity between all things,
     or almost all things, and in truth
as a glitter-ball throwing reflections here and there;
     in the impossibility of proof.
But this is the month when hours in a day are short,
     when the last and final word
comes only minutes after the first, and the strongest voice
     is the only voice to be heard,
and the nod of a head gets a squaddie on stand-by
     out to the kill-zone
for a weekend break in the sun, then spirited back to base
     before the postcards arrive home.
Whoever it was that said civilization is only one meal deep
     might have added that however far
we think we might have come, we are still only
     one word away from war.
And there are always at least two sides to every story,
     but when two sides say they are trying
to do what must be done for the best in the eyes of their God
     they could both be lying.
Back on the box, a graphic comes up on the screen:

Britain as an aircraft carrier
moored off the coast of continental Europe, home to a squadron
        of hawks and harriers
lifting from the flight-decks of Lincolnshire and Norfolk;
        either that, or St Nicholas
bent double with the heavy pillow-case of peace in Ireland,
        slouching towards Christmas.
They won't be removing the iron railings and metalwork
        from the school yard and the park gates
to melt down for bombs, but the Russians have called back
        their man in the States, and it is dark
to the East, dark until the bell goes or the cock crows,
        and the thing we were told
was a thing of the past is coming up once more like the dawn,
        and it is dark, and it is cold.

One has to recognize the business acumen
of high-street fashion houses.
This year's hottest duds are khaki body-warmers, anything
in camouflage, and combat trousers.

Meanwhile, a British broadcasting corporation is advertising
        for thirty volunteers
from all walks of life to be left to their own devices
        for twelve months
with nothing more than a Swiss Army knife each
        and a week's SAS training.
The hand-picked castaways will be set down on the shingle beach
        of some lost Scottish island
among a population of rabbits and several billion midges
        and given free licence
to go it alone for a year, either by building bridges
        with fellow Robinson Crusoes
or turning their backs on any form of civilization.
        Documentary bulletins
and video diary entries will be broadcast to the nation
        at regular intervals
on prime-time television, with a celebrity voice-over
        narrating the story
from original selection to the final shot of a helicopter
        airlifting bearded survivors
back to family and friends crying on a rain-swept harbour.
        As well as demonstrating
the thin line between paradise and hard labour,
        this millennial production
will observe how human society adapts and evolves,
        how basic problems are approached,
and how huge differences in personality are finally resolved.
        Thought-provoking and true,
from this microcosm of life we might be able to tell
        not just how society formed
but something of the future too. Also, it will be funny as hell.
        When it comes to selection,

nobody wants to play God, but for the sake of audience figures
        the series should reflect
a cross-section of contemporary life, and will no doubt feature
        some jockstrap from Loughborough
shouting the odds about teamwork and rules right from the off;
        some doctor from Gloucester
who goes down on day one with chilblains and whooping cough;
        some mealy-mouth veggie
caught on camera sucking marrow from a rabbit bone;
        some crusty new-ager
heard gassing with the Mother Goddess on a mobile phone;
        some chartered accountant
with steamed-up glasses who comes good in the end;
        some copper who can't hack it;
some loser in search of himself who goes round the bend;
        some pig-tailed professor
whose beautiful equations look wonderful written in sand
        but don't keep the rain out
or bring sea-trout writhing from salt-water to dry land;
        some interior designer
whose basket-woven birchwood lean-to is a work of art
        and kick-starts
a taste for survivalist sculpture and winds up in the Tate;
        some vicar whose dog-collar
stays white and starched throughout; some saint whose halo slips;
        some rough diamond
who cries like a baby at long last; some librarian who flips;
        some quiet type
who gets on with turning his land and sowing his seed,
        whose pot plants turn out
to be a particularly aromatic variety of weed;
        a butcher, a baker,

a candlestick maker, some cook, some thief, his wife
        and her lover,
basically a wide range of appealing stereotypes
        from those who want to own land,
take control, capitalize on every opportunity, and have wars,
        to those who want nothing
except peace, happiness, and to run around on all fours.
        Those interested in applying
should be warned that depression will almost certainly follow
        and that such a life-changing event
could leave even the most solid person feeling hollow
        and possibly suicidal,
although a highly trained team of counsellors will be available
        for any participant
showing signs of ill-health or becoming mentally unstable,
        counsellors with a track record
in working with freed hostages and survivors of torture.
        Also, with suffering being
what it is today — the new heroism — fame and fortune
        are practically guaranteed,
so agents will be watching with interest, as will lawyers
        and loss-adjusters.
Applicants are also advised that as responsible employers
        the corporation will carry out
thorough interviews and tests, and it can be taken as read
        that candidates will be the subject
of rigorous investigation and police checks. A spokesman said:
        a project that sets its sights
on nothing less than mimicking the evolution of the human race
        couldn't simply go ahead, willy-nilly,
without planning or putting certain safety measures in place.

More and more people are climbing mountains in Iceland
     these days. It's hard work,
but think of the view, the fresh air, the world at your feet;
     think of Björk.

Meanwhile this wintermonth, lives are boxed between the bounds
of Daylight Saving Time
like actors trapped by Cinemascope, and we do whatever we do
between two black borderlines.
Darkness waits to mug the postman, follows the heels of children
home from school,
and the sun comes only at midday to shave its beard
in the frozen pool,
rest its chin on the bald hill for a short afternoon.
Long nights and pinhole days.
In the small hours the brain dilates, free-wheels without fuel
from the sun's rays,
and the mind floats up to fill the emptiness of the universe.
The likes of us can wait;
others have deadlines and dates, and those who see as far
as Heaven's Gate
are said to be slipstreaming now through outer space
in the after-burn of an iceball
like a message in a bottle thrown from the *Titanic*.
But come nightfall,
the only foreign body in the sky is making for Heathrow,
and even if we raised our vision
well above the orange sodium of Earth's reflected glory,
the only space mission
likely to catch the milk-bottle lens of a star-gazing eye
is the flash of light
from an unmanned Russian mirror, sending back acres of sun
to contradict night
in certain northern black-spots, illuminate the lives
of seasonally disordered folk
whose power stations binge on gas or oil or timber,
coal or coke,

who move in a downcast world, whose only hope
        is to see in the dark
without night-vision military binoculars or a torch.
        Apparently carrots don't work.
So a barn owl draws the clouds of its wings
        over the world of its face,
and a fox marks time in its lair, and bats hang fire
        at the mouth of a cave,
and horses come to their half-open stable doors
        to look for their dreams,
and a phoenix is shot as it touches down to sip
        from the molten stream
next to the bodies of white harts, griffins, unicorns,
        dodos and great auks
as a marksman reloads in his hide, both barrels of his nostrils
        thick with smoke,
his sniper's eye telescopically wide, like a big fish potted
        in a small glass bowl,
his sight a kaleidoscope pie of bird, beast, fish and fowl,
        killed at the watering hole.
Every country has its own stroboscopic story.
        In Australia's southern reaches,
sunstroke breaches the fontanelle of the ozone hole
        and the crowds on the beaches
practise the slip, slap, slop of shirt-sleeves, headgear
        and plaster-cast sun-block,
then comb their skin at dawn for mole hills, fairy-rings,
        craters and sun-spots.
Here in the West on the bullied pistes of Alpine slopes,
        high above the tree-line,
no amount of long-range forecasting, dynamite and fair warning
        can stop ground-frost and sunshine

providing avalanche conditions straight from the manual,
    and when one snowboard
unhooks the safety-curtain from a mountain's shoulder
    it instantly downloads
enough whiteness to draw a veil over a matchstick village,
    snuff out its streetlight candles.
On home ground, a sky-diving stunt-parachutist over Villa Park
    looking to land centre-circle
falls like Icarus out of the sun and onto the terrace,
    announcing the new season,
and when the floodlights at several premiership grounds
    for no apparent reason
conk out midway through indifferent first-class fixtures,
    suspicion falls
not on a five-amp fuse or a three-pin plug or the National Grid,
    or the burn-out of fossil fuels,
but on those with a stake in the game, those hedging their bets
    in former far-east colonies
and other lands where the sun has suddenly come to set
    on former sunrise economies.
It's the world hotting up, they say, but it's hard to react;
    here in the driving seat
the car still wears a cataract of frost at first light,
    and here on easy street
banana skins of ice still do the trick, and here on the line
    washing freezes between pegs:
an armour-plated shirt, a pair of freeze-dried boxer-shorts,
    two iron legs,
petrified socks cocooned in cold. They hang
    like Mother Shipton's thoughts,
like Mother Shipton's moth, except each article of cloth
    comes true, of course, and thaws.

Tonight's the night for you couples intent on conceiving
    the new Christ.
Just do it, then lie back and dream about naming
    your own price.

Meanwhile, hot air rises.
And the two men held for twenty-one days in living conditions
      decidedly worse
than those in most high security prisons
      are not the victims
of some hard-line, oppressive regime, or political refugees,
      or eco-warriors
digging in on the side of rare toads and ancient trees,
      or dumbstruck hostages,
or Western tourists kidnapped by gun-toting terrorists,
      or moon-eyed murderers
on death row, or self-captivated Turner Prize exhibitionists,
      but balloonists, actually,
jet-streaming the globe, riding the one, continuous corner
      of the world's orb.
In a picnic basket swinging from a bunsen burner
      suspended beneath
a tuppeny rain-hood filled with nothing but ether,
      Messrs Piccard and Jones
hitched a ride on a current of air and lapped the equator
      in less time than it takes the moon
to go through its snowball-cycle of freezing and thawing.
      Think of all the mental energy
and tax dollars pumped into that Stealth bomber thing
      with its invisible paint
and silent engines and non-reflective angles;
      all that fuss
when all along we could have sided with the angels.
      All we have to do,
apparently, is catch the breeze and hold our breath,
      strike a match
and watch the planet going round and round beneath.

All right, in practice
it wasn't a cakewalk. Stowed away within the microclimate
of the capsule
was at least one mosquito that drew blood from both pilot
and co-pilot,
and one of the two had to spacewalk the outside of the canopy
snapping off icicles,
and not for Scotch on the rocks but as a matter of buoyancy.
Nevertheless, could those men
who emerged stunned and smelly, who were hoping to land,
touchingly, in the lap
of the Sphinx, rather than being dragged through sand
to the back of beyond,
could they be representative of some higher and finer ideal?
We could do worse,
couldn't we, than balloon? Could do worse than peel
the skin from the soul
and dither and drift in the miles of airspace between heaven
and Earth, could do worse
than quit the sink estates and the island tax-havens,
look down cartographically
on town and country, golf-blight and deforestation,
the veins and arteries of roads,
the blood-clots of traffic lights and service-stations.
Could do worse, surely,
than clink glasses, balloonist to balloonist, mid-air,
over invisible borders,
over East Timor, Rwanda, Eritrea,
catch the breeze
and exchange personal gifts as tokens of good fortune,
thrown basket to basket.
Forget flags on sticks, dolls in national costume.

We could do worse
than idle, unprotestingly, where jets might otherwise fly,
lounge on the flightpaths,
occupy no more than one balloon's-worth of sky, and not be tied
to any plot of land.
We could do worse, could we not, than only cool and drop
for supplies and fuel,
scoop snow with bare hands from mountain tops,
make fingertip friends
in passing, occasionally jump ship to have sex or make love
and generally
rise like thought bubbles without words into worlds above,
be aerial and detached
over Kosovo, Pristina, let the wind be the driving force,
let each bauble and blimp
be free and etherial, find its own way, follow its own course,
could do worse
than tilt in the frozen light above the weather
and every night
be part of the solar system, blissfully clear-headed, whatever
the state of play on the ground.
Be quiet and listen. From up there in the gods
a person can hear
a nightjar winding its watch for morning, contented bullfrogs
farting and snoring.
Balloons, like kindly, fat maiden-aunts in their new frocks
walking home from a wedding,
like the cows coming in, the sighting of slow, gentle yachts.
We could do worse
than hang around up there, thoughtful and vacant at once,
while all unstable elements lapse
to a steady state, while gaps and partitions are given the chance
to meet and mend,

while wounds heal, battlefields go to pot, weapons to rust.
  Impossible of course,
but couldn't we just, couldn't we just?

Scarborough beach on Good Friday, sandwriting
    says *Jesus is Lord*.
Letters come and go. On Sunday he's lard, lurid, blurred.
    By Tuesday he's bored.

Meanwhile, somewhere in the state of Colorado, armed to the teeth
     with thousands of flowers,
two boys entered the front door of their own high school
     and for almost four hours
gave floral tributes to fellow students and members of staff,
     beginning with red roses
strewn amongst unsuspecting pupils during their lunch hour,
     followed by posies
of peace lilies and wild orchids. Most thought the whole show
     was one elaborate hoax
using silk replicas of the real thing, plastic imitations,
     exquisite practical jokes,
but the flowers were no more fake than you or I,
     and were handed out
as compliments returned, favours repaid, in good faith,
     straight from the heart.
No would not be taken for an answer. Therefore a daffodil
     was tucked behind the ear
of a boy in a baseball hat, and marigolds and peonies
     threaded through the hair
of those caught on the stairs or spotted along corridors,
     until every pupil
who looked up from behind a desk could expect to be met
     with at least a petal
or a dusting of pollen, if not an entire daisy-chain,
     or the colour-burst
of a dozen foxgloves, flowering for all their worth,
     or a buttonhole to the breast.
Upstairs in the school library, individuals were singled out
     for special attention:
some were showered with blossom, others wore their blooms
     like brooches or medallions;

22

even those who turned their backs or refused point-blank
        to accept such honours
were decorated with buds, unseasonable fruits and rosettes
        the same as the others.
By which time a crowd had gathered outside the school,
        drawn through suburbia
by the rumour of flowers in full bloom, drawn through the air
        like butterflies to buddleia,
like honey bees to honeysuckle, like hummingbirds
        dipping their tongues in,
some to soak up such over-exuberance of thought, others
        to savour the goings-on.
Finally, overcome by their own munificence or hay fever,
        the flower-boys pinned
the last blooms on themselves, somewhat selfishly perhaps,
        but had also planned
further surprises for those who swept through the aftermath
        of broom and buttercup:
garlands and bouquets were planted in lockers and cupboards,
        timed to erupt
like the first day of spring into the arms of those
        who, during the first bout,
either by fate or chance had somehow been overlooked
        and missed out.
Experts are now trying to say how two apparently quiet kids
        from an apple-pie town
could get their hands on a veritable rain-forest of plants
        and bring down
a whole botanical digest of one species or another onto the heads
        of classmates and teachers,
and where such fascination began, and why it should lead
        to an outpouring of this nature.
And even though many believe that flowers should be kept

in expert hands
only, or left to specialists in the field such as florists,
the law of the land
dictates that God, guts and gardening made the country
what it is today
and for as long as the flower industry can see to it
things are staying that way.
What they reckon is this: deny a person the right to carry
flowers of his own
and he's liable to wind up on the business end of a flower
somebody else has grown.
As for the two boys, it's back to the same old debate:
is it something in the mind
that grows from birth, like a seed, or is it society
makes a person that kind?

Film footage of world history is a tracking shot
    along railway lines.
Here come the latest, gypsies sleepwalking between iron rails
    through acres of landmines.

Somewhere in the real world a girl asleep in a glass coffin
    cries occasional tears of blood,
and because that coffin is parked in the aisle of a church
    and not under a big top, she is good.

Meanwhile, the future waits at signal 109. And up ahead
    the wires will cross again,
and lines will cross at any given point, like a train
    bisecting a train,
and lives will be seen to be measured in pounds and pence,
    human worth as hard cash,
and Carriage H will hide its secrets in its ghostly freight
    of warm, weightless ash,
and mobile phones will call repeatedly across the great divide
    to lives already lost,
and cars in car-parks back along the track will keep for winter
    under sheets of frost.

This season, luggage containing terrible thoughts
was left in Brixton, Soho and Brick Lane,
the kind which scatters the baggage of one man's mind
into the public's brain.

Sixty-five per cent of all North American people
    are now officially obese.
Elsewhere, in countries closer to the sun, many thousands
    are still doing the ultimate striptease.

Why don't we start again from the top, from the head:
    dream up a new cult, think of a new force.
Time collects. Time passes, but not with the tread
    of footprints in sand or tyres along a road
or a train on the East Coast line, passing a junction box.
    Time collects, accumulates, gathers together,
remains to be seen. Time thickens, coagulates, clots;
    what lies at your feet is its sediment,
piled from the core to the surface, forming the ground.
    Time builds up in layers: up there
is the clean, unknowable future waiting to rain down
    or fall out, waiting to drop. The present,
the here and now, extends from our minds to our toes,
    from the crowned heads to the down-at-heel,
from verrucas to brain tumours, haloes and frontal lobes,
    from our snoods to our air-cushioned soles.
But underground is the past. Below stairs —
    that's where dust and bone
and pollen and skin and rust and soot and fibre and hair
    and splinter and soil are packed hard,
becoming stone, becoming rock, becoming earth.
    And not just things we can measure
and weigh, items of proof, material worth,
    but sounds and visions,
echoes and views — they lie here in the stone,
    jammed into silence
and blackness by time, by its billion billion tons,
    time laying down its load.
The great geology of time. The gravity of loss.
    And memory lies here too.
Memory — the glue of time, bonding it close,
    the gel that splices

one split second to the next, the gum that sets the past
        in solid form, binding it shut,
holding it monumentally hard and fast.
        So history can be opened again,
but not by force. Plastic explosive will fail
        to worm time from its shell;
hard labour, hammer blow, pulverization, blade and file,
        reduction of solid form to its powdered state
will not release time, neither will high-voltage connections,
        magnets, particular wavelengths of light,
nor pinning-down under powerful lenses, looking at sections slice
        by slice, or baking hard in a kiln.
Time will not be extracted like ore
        from its mother-rock, like mercury
from cinnabar, or drilled from the planet's core.
        Only water will work.
Water that makes its way down, reaches back to the first.
        Water which mimics the action of time,
which makes for the lowest point; that is its task, its thirst.
        The world over, water is working
its trick: conjuring up whatever is unseen and unsung.
        Atoms of history boil up
into the air, vaporize into the lungs.
        Hold it there. You are keeping
yourself in breath with the dates and figures and facts
        and lives and losses and loves
of a history smothered by dust. You are breathing the past.
        Make it real again, because
this is the cycle to which we are all born.
        We journeyed ashore
to set the past free, to release the secret of time from stone,
        uncurl the stubborn fist of what is gone,

to flood the rocks that hold the limited supply of time,
     to irrigate memory
and float the great, revolving permanence of humankind.
     Look down at your feet, which are fish.
Imagine everything locked in time's keep,
     everything buried, enshrined, encrypted, encoded, entombed
in sleep. Now, bring back the dead. Breathe deep.

Some passenger-seat friend of mine sometimes screams
    Red-line it, red-line it,
meaning get the revolutions of your life into that area
    beyond the upper limit.

Meanwhile, because more people worship the sun these days
        than God, millions flock
to England's toe-end, to see for themselves the great blaze
        turning a blind eye,
to stand in the shade of a satellite moon as it casts
        a shadow of doubt
over the South West, over modern lives. The spectacle lasts
        no more than a minute
or two, but St Ives is Bethlehem at census time, and the Lizard
        is Glastonbury all over again,
its hedgerows crawling with druids and witches and wizards
        and other occult sects,
and on Goonhilly Downs the tracking devices are one and the same
        with the city
of tents, marquees, and every make and type of canvas home
        to have mushroomed overnight,
and the surfers on Fistral Beach are gathered in praise
        of the tide,
and bandwagons — from banana buses to brewer's drays —
        are coming along for the ride.
So ruptured silage bags are dumped by farmers in passing places
        and tractors parked in gateways
to stop those with out-of-town accents or alien faces
        setting up camp
without paying the going rate for basic sanitation facilities.
        Every beach has its bum.
Every standing stone has its own Saint Simeon Stylites.
        Elsewhere in Britain,
to the flat east and the far north, across zones of partiality,
        even those landlocked
by work or home still want, if they can, to be part of it all,
        so inmates at Strangeways

get an extra turn of the exercise yard at the appointed hour,
      and shop-girls on elevenses
smoke Benson & Hedges down to the quick outside office doors,
      and MPs in the Commons
take to the terrace, leaving the country to freewheel
      for a moment or so,
and shop-fitters under the lid of the Dome down tools
      and prise off their hard hats
for the sake of the view, and suspects are taken downstairs
      while jurors in Norfolk
adjourn to the courthouse roof for a glimpse of the stars,
      and in Gateshead
motorists pull off the road to wait at the Angel's feet,
      and the Highlands and Islands
incline to the south for a second, detecting a fall in heat.
      Come the eleventh hour
and the eleventh minute, life-forms in distant galaxies,
      if they exist,
staring through space, now find us a strange species:
      millions of us,
our upturned faces wearing aluminium-coated glasses
      or welding masks,
armed with a billion candle-power of camera flashes
      or wielding home-made
Blue Peter-type optical devices, or spreading picnic blankets
      under the projection
like moonrakers, hoping to snaffle a star or planet
      by bagging its reflection.
Millions of us, all craning heavenwards, blindly gazing
      into the heart
of space, rubbernecking the single most amazing
      incidence of . . . dark.

In the event, the obvious happens. A consignment of grey sky
        treading water all week
off the coast, waiting for clearance, is given the green light
        and rolls in to port,
weighs anchor over St Michael's Mount, overshadowing the county.
        Rain follows quickly.
Naturally, bright sunshine floods the rest of the country,
        in varying degrees.
So nobody's eye gets fused to the sharp end of a telescope,
        as had been predicted;
where clouds do manage to part, a few films are over-exposed
        where filters should have been fitted.
Only from a plane flying well above the planet's ceiling
        does the full magnitude
of the total eclipse of the sun live up to its billing:
        dawn twice in the same day,
once from east, and once from the side where the sun usually sets;
        time running backwards;
the great black bird of the shadow, swooping from the west
        in total silence
at twice the speed of sound; first contact; corona;
        Baily's Beads;
prominences; diamond rings; totality; and the general aura
        you might reasonably expect
when one celestial body snookers another, when the sun blinks,
        when the great dimmer-switch
in the sky goes the whole way, and the man on the moon winks
        a black, lazy eye.
Some of the blessed and lucky and rich manage a snapshot,
        some said a lighthouse
tricked into doing its stuff was as good as it got,
        but for those on the ground

it was dark and cold and it rained. Full stop. Nevertheless
    it's a theory of mine
that those who went home chilled, gloomy, wet and depressed
    still got the message
loud and clear, and that what each individual truly felt
    was a huge sense of time
and space, and subsequently a loneliness bordering on guilt
    despite standing
shoulder to shoulder within the biggest human jamboree
    since the year dot.
Consequently, won't all those lonely souls now feel the need
    to get along,
resolve themselves to a life of having to come together
    whether they like it or not,
or at least as a race stop beating the shit out of each other
    remorselessly from one century
to the next, if only to try and make use or sense
    of what time we have left,
bearing in mind the complete absence of anything else?
    It was only a thought.
Or how about this: no matter how much bluster and hype
    went into the thing,
that old sun-and-moon trick sieved people into two types:
    those who stayed indoors
in artificial light and buried their brains in a book,
    and those who went and stood
within the clockwork of the solar system as it wheeled about
    and struck.

My solar-powered watch is on the blink again,
    this timepiece I truly worship;
either I'm wearing longer cuffs these days that block the light
    or it's the weather, going pear-shaped.

But, beloved,
be not ignorant of this one thing, that one day
    is with the Lord
as a thousand years, and a thousand years as one day.
    Meanwhile, with hyper-link text,
the interactive Domesday Book available on CD ROM,
    or in ten gilt-edged editions
from http://www.nicetolookatbutyou'llneverread'em.com;
    King Canute in China,
cutting the tape on a dam wall holding an ocean at bay;
    Harold at Hastings,
seeing the point of an Exocet missile coming his way.
    Robert the Bruce
looping the loop and walking the dog with a yo-yo;
    Dick Whittington on the street,
flogging the *Big Issue* from an office doorway in Soho.
    John Cabot winched by helicopter
from an upturned fibreglass hull in the north Atlantic;
    Sir Francis Drake rolling out
on green baize with perfect obovoids of moulded plastic.
    Chaucer at his laptop,
auto-checking his screenplay proposal for spelling and style;
    Guy Fawkes lighting up,
driving a lorry-load of fertilizer into the Square Mile.
    Scott selling hot dogs
and soft-scoop ice cream from a Dormobile at the South Pole;
    raising an eyebrow
at the Stephen Lawrence enquiry, Sir Robert Peel.
    James Watt fiddling the leckie,
running a three-bar fire from a lamp outside in the street;
    Captain James Cook
in Qantas Business Class, snoozing at thirty-thousand feet.

Emmeline Pankhurst in this year's
radical shake-up at BBC Radio 4, dropped by *Woman's Hour*;
Sir Donald Campbell
in a pedalo on Windermere with his foot flat to the floor.
Hitler on *Oprah*,
Stalin on *Esther*, Attila the Hun on *Celebrity Squares*.
Pope John Paul
being Pope John Paul being Pope John Paul, for a thousand years
in thy sight are but
as yesterday when it is past, and as a watch in the night.
Meanwhile, Easter Island statues
at the world summit; Sir Walter Raleigh in Spud-U-Like;
Edward the Confessor
dragging an altar-stone into the heart of the Dome;
Michelangelo, tagging a train
with spray paint in a railway siding outside Rome.
Shakespeare making
an arse of himself for Children in Need or *Sesame Street*;
the Earl of Sandwich in Burger Land,
chewing over his first genetically-modified sesame seed.
Florence Nightingale
dabbing the wounds of a face-lift patient in Beverly Hills;
Mother Teresa clued up
on Girl Power, breast implants and anti-cellulite pills.
John Logie Baird connected to cable,
flicking between log-rolling, tractor-pulling and topless darts;
Presley coming last
in an Elvis look-a-like contest for not looking the part.
Armstrong sunk in his thoughts,
singing hey-diddle-diddle and bringing back lumps
of the Berlin Wall
from the dark side of the moon on a London bus;
Bill Gates fitting a window,

cutting his hand on a leading edge of bulletproof glass.
      Hawkins and Dawkins on the case,
Hawkins fingering Christ through the garden fence,
      Dawkins dipping his dabs
into the hole in Jesus' side, looking for hard evidence
      and facts.
But, beloved, be not ignorant of this one thing, that one day
      is with the Lord
as a thousand years, and a thousand years as one day.

This is the Computer World Software Helpline, please
make sure you can see your screen.
Your call is being charged at two pounds fifty-five per minute,
my name is Gary, I'm thirteen.

Meanwhile on the Thames, attempts to hoist the BA London Eye
     have broken down,
reminding us of the difficulties in getting such pies in the sky
     off the ground.
Some say it's a giant water-wheel that turns with the tide,
     driving the country onwards,
some say it's nothing more than an overblown fairground ride
     piped up to the Commons,
powered by hot air and other parliamentary emissions.
     Some say the money
should have been spent on hospitals, schools or even prisons
     and have called it a scandal,
others see the sense in trying to raise people's sights
     above street level. Certainly
it's a hell of a drop from the fairy lights at the dizzy heights
     to rock bottom.

Flowers again at the accident black-spot this morning
and crumbs of windscreen glass.
And the people bring hubcaps as wreaths to lay on the roads
whenever the petals crash.

Meanwhile, on deck, the waiters clear the muddied plates,
    the scattered knives and forks.
A silver spoon collects the constellations in its palm.
    Too many to count, the corks
from bottles, magnums, jeroboams of champagne are eased loose
    by men who make a point
of doing nothing of the sort except to change a fuse
    or carve the Sunday joint.
Water laps against each prow. It's the eve of the dawn
    of the year two thousand.
Thousands make a chain of boats across a dateline further east,
    thousands wait on a far-east island.
Then the Chinese whisper of a countdown spreads across the crowd,
    first to be lit by a century's morning,
mad to say they were there and then when the moment came,
    wild for starlight that passes for meaning.
Time — as measured by a stopwatch, from a starting place.
    Below the dateline, fathoms deep,
where anchored chains won't reach, a fault-line on the seabed
    cracks and separates and weeps;
new rocks record the Earth's magnetic field, contentedly.
    And mollycoddled in the warmth,
old life-forms well below the register of sun, swayed
    by the moon's persuasive force,
go on regardless, blind, impelled, instinctively
    and unbeknown.
The moment comes . . . and goes. In surface water,
    corks that were blasted and blown
begin a slow, diverse migration out to distant shores,
    and foam and fizz and froth
that overshot each glass now pops, falls flat and dissipates,
    like last night's bubble bath.

Some people could have guessed. In irrelevant valleys
        and insignificant vales,
on pointless hills and featureless stretches of heath,
        on paths and trails
not aimed at ancient sites or aligned with patterns of stars,
        at grid references
where nothing really matters, along compass bearings
        of no consequence,
at spot heights without coincidence, in meaningless buildings
        and godless zones,
in the living-rooms, kitchens, bedrooms of commonplace houses
        and everyday homes,
a million souls are focused on keeping themselves to themselves,
        determined to opt out,
not to be moved by a fictional date and a fictional time,
        so many in fact
that those with an ear to the floor and an eye on the watch,
        taking the world's pulse,
listening for some stutter in the ticking of the solar clock,
        for a heartbeat missed,
some distant tremor like the splitting of the polar cap,
        detect instead
a silence so profound it figures on the Richter scale,
        as if the dead
from every age had risen from their hundred billion graves
        to speak a word
so soundlessly and noiselessly, that even in deep space
        it was heard.

Red sky at night — shepherd's delight; red sky
    in the morning —
too much to drink again trying to free your mind
    from the brain it was born in.

Some aviary in the Balkans
suffered damage from a nearby blast;
eagles, buzzards, vultures and falcons
all flew the nest.

Plovers, knots and Slavonian grebes
were suddenly on the loose;
that jet shot down over Zagreb
was a beautiful barnacle goose.

An ostrich legged it for cover,
skuas made for the pole star;
the story went round of a roadrunner
overtaking an armoured car.

Catbird, lapwing, snipe and stilt,
shoveler, toucan and quail,
diver, dipper, dotterel, stint —
they all turned tail.

Love-bird, barn-owl, bustard and shrike,
barbet, moorhen and skylark,
roller, egret, cuckoo and kite
made the blue sky go dark.

Some were taken in as pets,
some were scragged for their coats,
some ended up in cooking pots,
some were chased for sport,

some were used as camouflage,
some were roasted on spears,

some were accused of espionage
and put on trial as spies,

some were released for target practice,
some were reduced to giblets,
some were branded parasites
and hung on gibbets.

The rest hid among pines and birches
or were torn apart by bombs. None
were returned to their rightful perches,
all except one.

The lyrebird is a funny old stick,
a sort of wooden hen,
that piles up branches and twigs and leaves
into a dome-shaped den.

Its feathers, striped in brown and white
are another claim to fame;
when raised, they resemble the instrument
that gives rise to its name.

But weirdest of all its features
are its voice-box and its ears;
for the lyrebird eavesdrops on other creatures,
then parrots what it hears.

Dogs, cats and other birds
are common impersonations;
echoes of chainsaws have also been heard
in woodland locations.

But when finally caught and put on the spot
by animal psychologists,
this particular lyrebird blurted out
an unusual sequence of sound-bytes:

boots marching on tarmac,
razor wire shredding the breeze,
the onward grinding of tank-tracks
through deserted streets,

orders given in a foreign tongue,
the smashing of locks and latches,
petrol poured from a petrol can,
the striking of matches,

glass popping from window frames,
appeals to the mercy of God,
the calling out of particular names,
the splutter of firing squads,

bombers flying in endless drones,
the sonic boom of jets,
the rupture of metal, the melting of stone,
the reiteration of threats,

landmines erupting underfoot,
a selection of human screams,
national anthems played on a loop,
a ghost-written victory speech.

All sounds were perfectly formed
and easily identified,

except for a sort of background drawl
that couldn't be recognized.

After hours of patient listening,
and rewarding the lyrebird with worms,
and some enhanced audio-imaging,
the sounds were at last confirmed:

that whir was a motorized camera,
that trill was a mobile phone,
that hum was a tape-recorder,
that purr was a dialling tone.

That interference jamming the air,
that babble of white noise,
that signal bending and burning the ears
was the radiation of news.

And finally, last week in a West Yorkshire village
        nothing happened at all.
An incident room is being set up at the scene,
        and security cameras installed.